WOW!
EVENTS
that Changed the World

EVENTS
that Changed the World

Philip Ardagh

Illustrated by Mike Phillips

MACMILLAN CHILDREN'S BOOKS

For all those who made
a difference.

First published 2000
by Macmillan Children's Books
a division of Macmillan Publishers Ltd
25 Eccleston Place, London SW1W 9NF
Basingstoke and Oxford
www.macmillan.com

Associated companies throughout the world

ISBN 0 330 48103 7

1 3 5 7 9 8 6 4 2

A CIP catalogue record for this book is available from the British Library.

Printed by Mackays of Chatham plc, Chatham, Kent.

CONTENTS

EVENTS!

Try to imagine a world where the American War of Independence never took place, so what we call the USA today is nothing more than part of the British Empire. Try to imagine a world where the Industrial Revolution never happened, so few of us live in towns or cities and most of us still work on farms to survive, or a world where slavery was never abolished and is an acceptable part of everyday life. Or a world that didn't go through the terrible loss and suffering of two World Wars . . . It's not easy, is it? That's because these are the events that have shaped our world into what it is today. In this *WOW!* book, we take a look at some of the most important prehistoric and historic events that changed the world. As for the events that will shape this new century and new millennium, who knows what they'll be? Perhaps they're unfolding right now. Perhaps you're a part of them.

PHILIP ARDAGH
2000

FIRE, FARMING AND THE WRITTEN WORD

AUGUST 1799, NEAR ROSETTA, EGYPT

Napoleon's French army has overrun Egypt, and Fort Julien is being hastily constructed by a battalion of his engineers on the site of old ruins. French officer Pierre Bouchard is supervising the destruction of an old wall when he spots a strange black stone, covered in inscriptions. Like nothing he's seen before, he reports it to his superior officer, General Menou. Realizing its possible importance, the General has the find transported to Alexandria. This is the Rosetta Stone: the key to cracking the code of ancient Egyptian hieroglyphs, one of the oldest and most mysterious written languages in the world.

FROM PREHISTORIC TO HISTORIC

One of the greatest events in the advancement of humankind is, without a doubt, when *Homo sapiens sapiens* (modern human beings) stepped from prehistory into history. Prehistory (literally, 'before history') means prehistoric times, as in prehistoric monsters (yup, dinosaurs) and, much, much, much later, prehistoric 'cave' men and women. So what exactly is history? What's the particular event separating it from prehistoric times? The answer is the development of writing, as we'll discover, but it was a long time coming. And what other prehistoric events changed our world along the way?

TERRIBLE LIZARDS

The first dinosaurs appeared in the world about 230 million years ago and after a momentous, catastrophic event – most likely a comet hitting the Earth and altering its atmosphere, blocking out the sun – they were wiped out about 65 million years ago. The world had been theirs for an amazing 168 million years. When you consider that the first upright-walking humanoid, called *Homo erectus*, only appeared about 1.8 million years ago and that the first true human beings – *Homo sapiens sapiens* – only evolved on Earth about 100,000 years ago, you realize how new we are to this planet of ours. The actual name 'dinosaur' itself is less than two hundred years old, dreamt up at a time when a real interest in their remains was starting. It was invented in 1842 by Briton Sir Richard Owen, from the Greek *deinos* meaning 'marvellous' or 'terrible' (take your pick) and *sauros* meaning 'lizard'.

MARVELLOUS

THE FIRST TRUE HUMANS

No one can say with 100 per cent certainty *exactly* when the first true humans evolved. 100,000 years can only be an approximate figure – and some experts now believe that they appeared before then – but about 100,000 years ago is a good starting point. *Homo sapiens sapiens* weren't the only human-like people around at that time, though. They shared the planet with a less brainy bunch called the Neanderthals (*Homo sapiens neanderthalensis*) but, whereas the *Homo sapiens sapiens* survived from then on, the Neanderthals died out. Although they'd been around before *Homo sapiens sapiens*, they disappeared about 30,000 years ago. Why? Because, back then, it was only the fittest, smartest and most organized who survived.

HUNTER-GATHERERS

In the beginning, *Homo sapiens sapiens* – whom I'm now going to refer to as 'people', because that's exactly what they were – were what experts call hunter-gatherers. No prizes for guessing how they got that name. They hunted animals and gathered fruit, berries and vegetables. They were always on the move, looking for more animals to kill and fruit to gather. Animals were not only a source of meat but their skins made good clothes and their bones and antlers could be used as tools and weapons too. But it was a hard, dangerous life. If you didn't die of hunger or disease a wild animal might get you first.

FIRE!

The discovery of fire must have been an unbelievably important event for prehistoric people. The only reason why it doesn't appear in the book *WOW! Discoveries that Changed the World* is because we know so little about it. It's the same with spoken language. We know that over time grunts must have become words and then sentences, but much of it is supposition (which is a big word for 'guesswork' – but 'guesswork' based on some pretty educated reasoning). The early humans' first encounter with fire – and what it could do – was probably as a result of lightning. Lightning strikes a tree. The tree catches fire. People go and investigate. They see that fire is bright. They feel that fire is hot. They see that it frightens away animals and discover that those animals caught and burnt by it have tasty, soft flesh which is much easier to tear off and chew than the raw meat they're used to. The next step is to keep feeding a fire so that they always have a source of flame for this newly discovered wonder, giving them light, heat, protection and cooking. Later, they discover a way of creating their own fire with a spark of flint.

10

A STUNNING IDEA

Then came an event so important yet so simple that, when you look back at it, it's incredible to think what an impact it had on absolutely everything that followed. After 89,000-ish years of people hunting and gathering and forever being on the move, people began to settle down and create farms. (That's 11,000 years ago: 100,000 − 89,000 = 11,000.) Interestingly, this was happening in different parts of the world amongst different people but at about the same time. Instead of people having to hunt animals for food, they bred animals in captivity so that they were there when they needed them. They took the biggest and best seeds and began to grow crops. People could stay put, and staying put meant that they could turn their attention to other things.

CREATING A COMMUNITY

Whereas, in the past, *everyone's* job had been to hunt or gather or both, not everyone on a farm needed to do the same job. Some people could look after the animals, others could look after the crops. Some people could make pots to hold the milk from the animals or store the seeds for crops. Others could turn their attention to keeping the gods happy, whilst some might commit themselves to designing better tools or making better clothes. Now that people were staying in one place, they needed proper homes, so a skill at building wood and mud houses developed. And people had time to decorate: make pictures, designs and patterns on objects around them. This was the beginning of real multi-skilled (lots of people with different talents doing different things) communities.

BASIC RECORD-KEEPING

Now that people were living together in these farming communities, it became necessary to start keeping basic records of who owned what. The most basic form of record-keeping was cutting a notch in a piece of wood, bone or antler for, say, each animal owned or each jar of corn stored. Once the numbers got very high, though, wouldn't it be easier to use a cross or a squiggle to take the place of a certain number of notches?

A NEW ERA FOR HUMANKIND

Then, just 5,500 years ago, these notches became more and more complicated and writing began to take shape. Then, sometime before 3000BC, the first true written language was developed in Sumer, Mesopotamia (which is now a part of Iraq) and was written on clay tablets with a pointy stick, not on paper.

GETTING BETTER ALL THE TIME

Rather than an alphabet, Sumerian writing was made up of symbols. In the beginning, these symbols were little pictures representing animals, plants and objects, including 'bird', 'sun', 'grain' and 'oxen' (all ideal for record-keeping). Over time, these pictures became simplified and stylized (looking less and less like the object they represented) until the symbols developed into cuneiform writing. 'Cuneiform' means 'wedge-shaped'. This is because the stick now used to press the writing onto the clay tablets was a special wedge shape.

EGYPTIAN HIEROGLYPHS

The Ancient Egyptians developed their writing about 100 years later and were possibly influenced by the Sumerians, though it might have developed separately. Over time, ancient Egyptian hieroglyphs became a highly complicated and sophisticated written language, covering monuments, walls, temples and scroll upon scroll of **papyrus**. So many examples of these hieroglyphs remain today that experts have been able to study them in great detail. There are over 6,000 separate glyphs (which is the name given to the symbols), and they have three different functions. Glyphs can be used as ideograms, phonograms or determinatives.

● With an ideogram, what you see is what you get. A glyph of an owl means owl!

- Phonograms represent sounds which, when put together, make up the sound of a word. This is how our alphabet works. For example, the letters 'd', 'o' and 'g' represent the meaningless sounds 'd-' '-o-' and '-g' but, when put together, mean that tongue-lolling, tail-wagging creature we know and love!
- Determinatives are the glyphs that go at the end of a word, helping the reader *determine* what the word is all about. (For example, the glyph of a seated woman at the end of a word means that the word has to do with a woman or girl.)

Ancient Egyptian had no gaps between words, didn't use **punctuation** and could be written left to right, right to left or top to bottom! And all of this was worked out and published by Frenchman Jean-François Champollion in 1824 thanks, primarily, to the Rosetta Stone. (Inscribed in hieroglyphics *and* Greek, it provided a way of translating hieroglyphics.)

THE ALPHABET

At the same time that the Egyptians were first writing in hieroglyphs, a system of writing, now called Proto-Elamite, was developed in Elam, in what is now Iran. Ancient Chinese developed about 1400BC. Each and every one of these languages was based, in some way or another, around picture symbols rather than a simple **phonic alphabet**. It was the Ancient Greeks who, in about 800BC – 2,800 years ago – developed a system of writing based solely on an alphabet. The advantage of such a system is that, in English, for example, you only need an alphabet of 26 letters to make up the 40-or-so sounds that go together to make up every single spoken word in the English language. In Chinese, however, where a phonic alphabet isn't used, you need to know about 3,000 characters to be able to read a newspaper from cover to cover.

STEPPING INTO HISTORY

And so we've reached the last big event in a chapter full of them. The dinosaurs have been wiped out, humans have appeared, they've discovered the use of fire and settled down to farm and to build communities, and now they have writing – and prehistory is at an end. Why? Because history means events that took place in a time when things could be written down and reported – a time when we no longer simply have to rely on archaeological evidence but can also study records written by human beings. In other words, in the 100,000 years that human beings have been on Earth, only events in about the last 5,500 years count as history, and that's less than 5.5 per cent of our time here!

THE RISE AND FALL OF ANCIENT ROME

15 MARCH 44BC, ROME

After being a **republic** for over five hundred years, Rome is
now being ruled by the 'dictator for life', Julius Caesar.
There are those who see him as a great soldier and a great
leader – a unifier of the people with the people's interests
at heart – and those who want to see a return to a republic
as quickly as possible, even if that means killing this man
who stands in its way. Julius Caesar should have listened to
those warnings and bad omens, for now he is ambushed
and stabbed repeatedly – twenty-seven times in all –
before falling dead to the ground. But the republic will
never return.

THE FOUNDING OF ROME

The first Romans got their
name from the city of
Rome, though they were
originally from a tribe
called the Latins (which is
why Romans spoke Latin).
The city grew up from
seven separate villages on
seven hills, which eventually merged
into one big city. No one knows for sure

when this happened, but legend has it that Rome was founded in 753BC, so it probably was round about then. The legend goes that a pair of abandoned baby boy twins, Romulus and Remus, were found by a she-wolf who brought them up and cared for them. When they were grown up, they planned to build a city on the spot where the she-wolf had found them. After a petty argument, though, Romulus killed his brother Remus so he built the city alone, became its sole ruler and called it 'Rome' after himself. The city of Rome is in the country we now call Italy, about six miles inland, on the River Tiber.

FROM FOREIGN KINGS TO A REPUBLIC

The city of Rome was originally in a region called Latium but wasn't just lived in by Latins. There were Etruscans (from the neighbouring region of Etruria) living there too. In fact, very early in its history – I'm talking well over 2,500 years ago here – the city of Rome found itself being ruled by Etruscan kings. The last one of these was said to have been kicked out in 510BC or 509BC. At that time, Rome declared itself an independent republic and nothing to do with the rest of Latium. The other cities in Latium (Alba Longa and Laurentum) didn't like this one bit, so joined forces to attack the Romans. At first, the Latium alliance had the upper hand but, by 400BC – after 100 years of fighting on and off – it was Rome that'd doubled the size of its territory and was now the most dominant power in the region.

THOSE GALLING GAULS

In 387BC, people from northern Europe, called the Gauls, invaded Rome. According to the Roman historian Livy (writing over 300 years later), most Romans fled, leaving just a few troops and the **senators**. To the utter amazement of the attacking Gauls, the Roman senators simply sat around in their garden courtyards looking as calm as calm can be. When one of the Gauls prodded a senator's beard to check he was real, the senator hit him with his stick! There was then a terrible massacre in which all the senators were killed and most of Rome was destroyed. Only the buildings on the Capitoline Hill (one of the seven) remained standing. Why? According to legend it was because geese in the temple on that hill heard the enemy coming under the darkness of night and honked in alarm. This gave those few Romans left in the city enough time to organize enough gold to bribe the Gauls to go away!

PYRRHIC VICTORIES

By 380BC, the Romans had rebuilt much of the city and added a wall around the seven hills. They also managed to regain their power in the Latium region, defeating the other cities in battle. There then followed forty years of war against the Samnites (326BC–286BC), in which the Romans not only defeated them, but also the Gauls and the Etruscans. Then, in 282BC, the Pyrrhic wars broke out. These were named after a person: King Pyrrhus of Epirus (in northern Greece). Although Pyrrhus defeated the Romans in 280BC and then again in 279BC, an enormous number of his soldiers were killed along the way. He's famous for having said, 'One more such victory and we'll be lost!' Today, the term 'Pyrrhic victory' refers to a victory won at too heavy a price. By 264BC, though, the Romans were the genuine victors and Rome was now the main power in Italy. The Latin language and Roman culture and influence spread right across the country.

THE THREE PUNIC WARS

Although the Romans were the top power in Italy, the top power in much of the western **Mediterranean** were the Carthaginians from the North African coastal city of Carthage. In 264BC, a series of wars broke out between the two peoples. The first Punic war – named after the Latin word for the Phoenicians, the founders of Carthage – lasted from 264BC to 241BC and was won by the Romans. They not only won lots of money off Carthage (a kind of payment for damages) but were also given the island of Sicily, their first territory

19

that wasn't part of Italy. A few years later, Rome seized Sardinia and Corsica too. The second Punic war (218BC–201BC) began when the Carthaginian General Hannibal famously brought his army of 35,000 troops and 37 elephants over the Alps to attack Rome! (Only one elephant made it. The other 36, along with 10,000 men, died along the way.) Despite this, Hannibal was an amazing General, winning victory after victory. In sixteen years of fighting though, he never conquered the city of Rome itself. In the end, the Romans conquered Carthaginian-ruled Spain. Now *they* were the top power in the western Mediterranean. The third Punic war (149BC–146BC) was much shorter than the others. Carthage itself was burnt to the ground by the Romans and the region became a Roman **province**! In 146BC the Romans also destroyed another city: Corinth, marking the beginning of Roman rule in Greece under a Roman **governor**. From 133BC to 31BC – that's over 100 years – the Romans took over most regions in the Mediterranean, all the way from Spain to Egypt.

FROM REPUBLIC TO EMPIRE

From the removal of the last Etruscan king in 510BC or 509BC to Julius Caesar – possibly the most famous Roman of all – becoming dictator in 44BC, Rome was technically a republic. From 146BC to 78BC, in particular, this republic was in crisis, with various attempts to wrench the power away from a citizens-elected senate. Caesar was appointed dictator for life in the February of 44BC but he was murdered just one month later, in an attempt to restore the republic, but this wasn't to be. After years of civil war, Julius Caesar's adopted son, Octavius, was made the first Emperor of Rome in 27BC and given the new name of Augustus. Now Rome was an empire.

EMPIRE AND CIVIL WAR

The empire grew and grew and – you guessed it – grew, until it was at its height (had its most territory) during the reign of Emperor Trajan, who ruled from AD98 to AD117. The trouble was, the bigger the empire became, the harder it was to control. There was a period in Roman history known as 'the Anarchy' 118 years later. After the murder of the emperor, an army leader called Maximus Thrax (a **barbarian**) was declared emperor, but he'd not only never set foot in Rome, he could hardly speak a word of Latin either! Not surprisingly there followed a series of civil wars. The Anarchy ended with the declaration of General Diocletian as emperor in AD284.

SPLIT IN TWO

Diocletian made a number of radical changes, including making the army bigger and responsible for the administration of the empire, and the provinces smaller

and easier to administrate. His biggest change, however, was to split the empire in two. He would rule the East and a man called Maximian would rule the West. It didn't stay this way for long. Diocletian and Maximian retired in AD305. Six years later, there were still four people squabbling for the right to rule.

THE CHRISTIAN CONSTANTINE

A soldier named Constantine defeated his main rival and become an emperor in AD312. He reunited the territories, turning them back into a single empire, with him as the sole Emperor of Rome from AD324 to AD337. He moved the capital of Rome away from the city of Rome in AD330 to the newly built city of Constantinople (named after himself, but now called Istanbul, in Turkey) and declared himself a Christian on his deathbed in AD337.

AND FINALLY

Thereafter, the empire was divided, united and divided again into east and west, with the barbarians attacking and overrunning various territories. AD476 saw Romulus Augustulus, the last emperor of Rome's Empire of the

West – named after Romulus the legendary founder of Rome – deposed by a German soldier, who declared himself to be king of Italy, thus completing the fall of the Western Empire. Meanwhile, the Empire of the East became known as the Byzantine Empire, a flourishing Christian empire, with Constantinople as its capital. Its most famous ruler was Justinian (AD527–565), who managed to reconquer much of the Rome's old territories in the west too. In AD1453 – that's good old 1453, as in just over 500 years ago – however, the Muslim Turks conquered Constantinople and any remaining links with the Roman Empire, founded way, way back in 27BC were broken.

Since they ruled so much of the world for such a long time, the Romans' influence on all aspects of life is immense. They brought towns and cities to many countries which had previously only known village and country life. Their long, straight roads influenced later road-builders and even, some say, railway-builders. (The gauge, or wheel-width, of many railways is 143 cm – apparently the fixed width of Roman wagons, designed so their wheels would fit in the ruts that built up in the roads.) Later, influential architects followed the Roman design for buildings, whilst artists copied their paintings and sculptures, particularly during the **Renaissance**. Ideas of Roman law and government also survive around the world today, and then there is the Roman language, Latin, the basis for many words in many languages, including English. The stamp Ancient Rome has left on the world is almost impossible to calculate (from the Latin word *calculus*, meaning 'a pebble used as a counter'). See what I mean?

THE INDUSTRIAL REVOLUTION

JULY 1815, SOMEWHERE IN CHESHIRE, ENGLAND

The meeting is a secret. Those gathered call themselves
'Luddites' after General Ned Ludd, the man who first
organized the movement back in Nottingham in 1811. But is
Ludd his real name? Does he exist at all? That doesn't
matter. What matters is the machinery that is being
introduced everywhere - the machinery which is doing the
work that men and women used to do. It must be smashed.
Destroyed. That's what this meeting is about: making final
plans before another attack on the new machines in a
textile mill. If they're caught, they could be **transported** or,
worse still, hanged. But the Luddites are prepared to stand
and fight. It's a lost cause. By 1816, they will all have
disbanded. Industrialization is here to stay.

A DIFFERENT KIND OF REVOLUTION

Not all revolutions involve people armed with makeshift
weapons storming palaces or freeing prisoners from
jails, or even men with large moustaches firing revolvers in
the air. The word 'revolution' has other meanings. One is
'a drastic change in methods and ideas', and that's exactly
what the Industrial Revolution was: the changing of first
Britain, then western Europe and the USA into industrial
nations.

FARMING

Ever since our first farmers settled down 11,000 years ago (back on page 11), farming remained the backbone of all civilizations. People had to eat to live, so much of the land and a great deal of time and effort went into raising crops and animals for food. A rich medieval baron might have had fine castles and an army of knights wearing his **coat-of-arms** and fighting in his name, but he also needed plenty of land and serfs (labourers who couldn't leave the land they worked on) to farm it to keep him in his wealth. The Church too expected payment in the form of tithes – a percentage of the crops a person grew. To be really rich you needed to own a vast amount of land and to turn much of it over to food production. Land equalled riches. The Industrial Revolution was to change all of that.

AGRICULTURAL ADVANCES

The Industrial Revolution started at the beginning of the eighteenth century – in the early 1700s. It partly came about as a result of the Agricultural Revolution in Britain. Better farming practices and equipment was being invented, including everything from seed drills for planting, to bigger and more efficient ploughs. Farms themselves were being restructured with landlords renting land to farmers, who then paid labourers to work it. Suddenly, the same amount of land was producing much larger quantities of food. In other words, there was (what people who like to use big words would say) increased agricultural productivity. And what was the result of this? That even more people could be freed to work elsewhere.

INVENTION AFTER INVENTION

As well as people inventing machinery that could make the farmers' lives easier, people were also inventing machines that would revolutionize the manufacturing (making) of goods. In 1733, John Kay invented the **flying shuttle** which doubled the amount of weaving a weaver could do in a single day! In 1764, James Hargreaves's spinning jenny – a wheel which allowed one person to spin many different threads at once – could make a typical spinner spin sixteen times faster! Then, in 1769, Richard Arkwright developed something called the 'water frame' – which, powered by a watermill, pulled fibre from cotton and spun it into thread on a frame – completely revolutionizing the amount and quality of cotton twine and material produced. Meanwhile, the steam engine and locomotive went from strength to strength and iron production was improved and increased.

FROM COUNTRY TO TOWN

Suddenly, industries were beginning to use new and improved machinery which, with a big enough workforce to operate it, could lead to an increase in production beyond anyone's wildest dreams. This mechanization (use of machinery) led to the building of huge mills and factories, and of homes for the workers to live in. Before the Industrial Revolution, most people lived in towns and villages in the country, which are called 'rural communities'. In fact, in 1800 there was only one city in the whole world which had more than a million people living in it, and that was London. Now that people were leaving farming and the countryside to work in the factories, towns and cities – urban areas – grew and grew. By 1900, there were ten cities in Britain with populations of over a million and the world's urban population had tripled.

IMPROVED CONDITIONS?

This move to the towns would ultimately mean improved living conditions for most people, but it was a long while coming. Old farm workers' cottages in the countryside may look picturesque today but since they were unheated, unlit, leaky-roofed and without sanitation, many can't have been much fun to live in. A move to new purpose-built homes near a factory probably seemed like a dream come true to some people. Of course, there were problems of overcrowding and poor sanitation in these new urban developments, and some were little more than slums, often within the shadow of huge factory chimneys belching out black smoke . . . but things did get better eventually.

FROM LANDED GENTRY TO INDUSTRIALIST

Now a person could be rich without owning any farmland. He – and it was just about always a 'he' – could be a mill, steel foundry or factory owner. He was not a member of the landed gentry, whose land and wealth went back generations, but was an industrialist and a capitalist, making his money from the production and selling of goods. Many of this new class of person made their wealth on the backs of poorly paid workers. In the north of England, the main industry was cotton. The big new mills of the early nineteenth century meant that profits soared, but workers' wages remained the same. They had no share in this new-found wealth. Some industrialists, however, were great **philanthropists** and were keen to create excellent living conditions for their workers, encouraging education as well as good housing.

IRON ROADS OF THE REVOLUTION

The spread of the railways in the 1830s (which you can read about in *WOW! Inventions that Changed the World*) not only opened up whole new markets to these new **mass-produced** clothes and other goods, but also helped the growth of the iron and steel industry. Someone had to supply all the metal to make the machines and build the tracks. Then there were steam ships to be built too. Engineering industries were cropping up everywhere. The Industrial Revolution had quickly spread through France, Belgium, Germany, and the United States by the middle of the nineteenth century, and reached Sweden and Japan by the end. Industrialization then began in Russia, Canada and beyond in the twentieth century.

THAT'S SOME REVOLUTION!

So what were the effects of the Industrial Revolution on the world? Massive. It introduced new approaches and new technology, with the careful application of both practical and scientific knowledge to the manufacturing process. The Industrial Revolution, therefore, changed the whole nature of production – what was produced, where and how – and switched from production of primary products (such as corn) to the production of manufactured goods and services. There were now more manufactured goods than ever before. This revolution not only altered countries' economies but also their societies with large clusters of enterprises now located within vast towns and cities. Most revolutions of the overthrowing-the-government variety haven't achieved such world-wide changes as that!

THE AMERICAN WAR OF INDEPENDENCE

25 DECEMBER 1776, DELAWARE RIVER, NORTH AMERICA

No Christmas celebrations here. It is night and, under the cover of darkness and a terrible storm, General George Washington, the man who will one day become the first President of the United States of America, is leading a small army of just 2,500 men across the ice-choked river and on to victories against British forces at Trenton, and then at Princeton. News of these successes will boost the morale of the **American Patriots** fighting for their independence against their English masters.

A GROWTH IN SIZE AND DIFFERENCES

The American War of Independence (1775–83) was fought between the inhabitants of the thirteen British colonies and their 'masters' who laid claim to North America: the British. There were a whole variety of different reasons as to why the colonists finally had enough of their 'mother country'. For starters, the sheer number of colonists had grown beyond all recognition. The first colony was established in 1607. By 1700, there were about 250,000 colonists. By the 1770s there were ten times as many which, if my maths is any good, means 2.5 million of them! Not only that, far fewer of them had a British background than before. While the New England colonies of Connecticut, Rhode Island, Massachusetts, and New Hampshire were still very British in numbers of colonists and their way of life, most other colonies were made up of Europeans from elsewhere. There was also the fact that about 20 per cent of the population of the North American British colonies was now black, because of slavery. That's over 565,000 people. Understandably, they had absolutely no loyalty to Britain.

RELIGION

There was also a real mish-mash of different religious beliefs. Whereas the original Pilgrim Fathers who came from England – see *WOW! Discoveries that Changed the World* – were low church Protestants, the colonists had splintered into a variety of different Protestant groups over the years, and Roman Catholics and Jewish people had also settled there. What this meant for North America's British masters was that it was harder for them to please and control such a large number of people from such different backgrounds and with such different beliefs.

DIFFERENT COLONIES, DIFFERENT RULES

In the 1750s, a colonist's first loyalty was to his or her colony, not to Britain. Each colony had its own governor and law-makers. There were, by then, three types of colony: corporate, proprietary and royal.

- If you were a white, property-owning man living in a *corporate colony*, you could not only vote for who sat in the colony's assembly – all colonies had one – but also for the colony's governor and council members.
- In a *proprietary colony*, however, you weren't ruled by elected council members but by descendants of those who originally founded the colony. The governors were still chosen by the British.
- The *royal colonies*, which made up eight of the thirteen British colonies had governors appointed by the king, and – except for Massachusetts – the council members were nominated by the king-appointed governor and approved by the British Board of Trade.

There wasn't one policy making British governing body to affect all thirteen colonies, or to make the inhabitants feel a part of Britain.

THE ASSEMBLIES

Each colony, whatever its type, had its own assembly. While its British masters ruled on matters such as trade and foreign affairs, the colonists were pretty much left to their own devices when it came to local laws and taxes. The British thought that such fairness would leave the colonists contented, while what it actually did was to create an excellent **forum** for those colonists wanting to break free of Britain to have an independent North America. In the meantime, the British rather ignored the colonies, leaving the colonists to their own devices.

THE SEVEN YEARS' WAR

Then 1756 saw the outbreak of the Seven Years' War in North America – and no prizes for guessing when it ended. Yes, seven years later in 1763. It wasn't the colonists against the British but the British against the French. It wasn't so much a proper war as a number of separate skirmishes, centred mainly around the northern colonies. The British were eventually victorious and gained land in Canada and Florida, but the war had been expensive and they found themselves in debt. Who better to turn to for money than the British colonists? The British looked at North America with renewed interest, introducing new laws and taxes and reinforcing old ones. The colonists resented this heavy-handed interference.

STAMPING AUTHORITY

A whole series of British laws followed, declaring what the people of the North American colonies could and could not do. Then there was the much-loathed Quartering Act of 1765 which meant that colonists had to house, feed and supply British troops quartered (stationed) in their areas. In other words, they were expected to pay for and support what many of them considered to be an occupying foreign army! Worse was yet to come. The Stamp Act meant that colonists had to buy special revenue (tax) stamps and stick them on everything from legal documents and newspapers to playing cards!

GONE TOO FAR

Many colonists decided that enough was enough. Here they were having to pay British taxes drawn up by the British parliament without being able to vote for any MPs to represent them in that parliament. In other words, as their slogan put it, this was: 'taxation without representation'. In October 1765, delegates from nine of the British colonies met in New York for an anti-Stamp Act meeting called the Stamp Act Congress. They sent a petition to the king, George III, asking him to scrap the Act. Others colonists took more immediate drastic action, destroying stamps, forcing tax officials to resign and, in Boston, an angry mob even destroyed the home of the lieutenant governor, Thomas Hutchinson. Britain was losing its grip on the colonies.

NO TURNING BACK

Many British merchants wanted the Stamp Act repealed (scrapped) too. All this unrest was losing them trade with the colonists, and they wanted things to go back to the way they had been. Now more and more colonists were boycotting British goods. Unfortunately for everyone, rather than repealing the Act, a newly elected British government, under Lord Rockingham, confirmed that the British had the right to tax any of their subjects – which included the inhabitants of the thirteen British colonies in North America – whether they had the vote or not. So there. Yah boo sucks.

A TAX ON TEA

Despite Britain's attitude, a peaceful solution did seem possible as far as some of the colonists were concerned. American colonist Benjamin Franklin – who was such a general all-round amazing guy that he also appears in *WOW! Discoveries that Changed the World*, for his work on electricity – declared, in his role as statesman, in 1769 that Britain should: 'repeal the laws . . . recall the troops, refund the money . . .' A new British government, this time under Lord North, went some way towards easing the pressure. However, the troops remained and, to remind the colonists that the British could tax what they wanted whenever they wanted, they put a tax on tea. This led people from different colonies joining forces, and more and more people expressed their pride in being American.

THE BOSTON TEA PARTY

In November 1773, with the British tax on tea in force, three British ships arrived in Boston harbour with a cargo of 342 chests of tea in their holds. If they were unloaded, the colonists would have to pay duty (tax) on each chest. So the citizens of Boston refused to unload them. The governor of the colony of Massachusetts, however, refused to allow the ships to leave *until* they'd been unloaded and the duty paid. There was a stalemate – until, on the evening of 16 December, a group of colonists crept aboard the ships and tipped all the tea out of the chests and into the water. Led by the American Patriot Samuel Adams, many of them covered their identity by disguising themselves as Native Americans!

THE RIDE OF PAUL REVERE

Things swiftly moved from bad to worse. The assembly of the colony of Massachusetts was supposed to meet in Boston but began to meet illegally in Concord. In 1775, British troops were ordered to go to Concord, to close down the assembly and arrest the ringleaders. A group of American Patriots – including a man named Paul Revere, later made famous in a poem by Longfellow – rode through the night from Boston to Concord to warn them that the British were coming. The message got through (though, unlike the story told in the poem, Revere himself was stopped by the British) and the colonists were ready for the troops when they came. The troops retreated to Boston with over 270 casualties, whilst the Patriots lost less than a hundred people.

DECLARATION OF INDEPENDENCE

The colonists made one last attempt at peace, but the British would have none of it. They put a **naval**

blockade around the colonies so that no trade could go in or out. Englishman Thomas Paine, who settled in America, pointed out how ridiculous it was that a tiny island should continue to try to rule a huge continent! A 'Continental Congress' had been formed, made up of representatives from the various colonies on the North American continent and they chose a man named George Washington to lead the Continental Army. On 4 July 1776, they issued the Declaration of Independence, which explained the reasons for breaking away with Britain and declared that the colonies were now the free and independent United States of America.

PROS AND CONS

Mistakenly, the British believed that they could win this war with brute force. Not only did Britain have a huge army compared to the numbers the Patriots would be able to call up to fight, but there were also still those colonists in America loyal to the British cause, along with some Native Americans who'd never liked the colonists in the first place. The Americans, on the other hand, had the advantage of being familiar with the territory they were fighting on – they knew the lie of the land. Not only that, the Patriots later received funding from Britain's old enemies in America: France and Spain. But it was true to say that the American soldiers were few in number and very badly fed and clothed, and often never paid. No wonder there were often **mutinies** against the American Generals! But the longer they fought, the better organized they became and the more battles they won.

THE FOUR PHASES OF THE WAR

Looking back on the American War of Independence, war historians have divided it into four distinctly different phases: Phase One, from April 1775 to July 1776, was when the American Patriots managed to turn what started out as little more than a small rebellion into a full-scale revolution, with the British and **Loyalists** trying to keep them down. (The worst fighting between the Patriots and Loyalists was in the south where, for a while, civil war reigned. It was also during this first phase that the Patriots invaded Canada. Though failing to take Quebec, the American army became better organized during this part of their military campaign.) Phase Two began in July 1776 with a massive British invasion of New York and ended with a British defeat at Saratoga in October 1777 (seen by many as the real turning point in the war). Phase Three began at the start of the following year with British forces concentrating on seizing land in the south and leaving the Loyalists to defend it. At this stage, the Patriots used very effective guerrilla tactics against the British and, with the French, won a memorable victory against them in Yorktown, Virginia in October 1781. Phase Four, the final phase, was a time for American diplomacy.

WINNING THE PEACE

After the humiliating surrender of British troops at Yorktown, the British government was growing tired of war. They would have to raise taxes at home to support a further war effort and knew that this would be most unpopular with the voters. Although a few skirmishes continued here and there, the final two years of the war were taken up trying to sort out a peace acceptable to everyone. It was officially declared that Britain would no longer be involved in 'an offensive war in America' and the British government opened negotiations with the Americans – as I'll now call them – and their French allies. On 3 September 1783, the Treaty of Paris was signed, in which Britain kept Canada and won rights for British traders in America, and promises for the protection of Loyalists who'd fought alongside them in the war (in fact, 100,000 of them left America, taking their wealth with them). Britain now fully acknowledged the independence of the United States of America.

WORLD SUPERPOWER

It really goes without saying why the American War of Independence was such a world-changing event because, today, the USA is the most powerful country in the world. It had a long way to go to get there after 1783, from the writing of the Constitution to the swearing in of George Washington as their first president in 1789, through the American Civil War (1861–65) – with North against South, **Unionist** against **Confederate** –

the abolition of slavery and the struggles of the civil rights movement, through to the present day, but get there it did and is now the central country on the world stage.

THE RISE AND FALL OF THE SLAVE TRADE

OCTOBER 1854, SPRINGFIELD, ILLINOIS, USA

The young man standing on the speaker's platform is wearing no collar or tie and has his shirt sleeves rolled up in a business-like fashion. He is here to speak out against an act passed by the United States government which extends slavery when, in his opinion, it should be banning it. 'When the white man governs himself, that is self-government,' he says, 'but when he governs himself, and also governs another man – that is **despotism** . . . my ancient faith teaches me that "all men are created equal", and that there can be no moral right in connection with one man's making a slave of another.' The speaker's name is Abraham Lincoln. Less than seven years later, he will become the 16th President of the United States of America.

THE MOST TERRIBLE TRADE

The European trade in African slaves – kidnapped black African people who were snatched from their homes, shipped abroad and forced to work in often terrible conditions for no pay – lasted for almost 400 years, during which time a staggering 15 million slaves were taken to the Americas – North and South – to work on plantations on land belonging to the various empires. Millions more died in the vessels, nicknamed 'coffin ships', that were supposed to take them there. Slavery is one of the worst examples of human beings' inhumanity to human beings, but it wasn't until the late eighteenth century that the anti-slavery movement was born.

THE BIRTH OF SLAVERY

Slavery goes back to the earliest civilizations with slavery common in ancient Egypt, Greece and Rome. The spread of Roman power meant that slavery went with it and, right up until the eleventh century, slavery still existed in Britain. Even in the 'New World', Mayan, Inca and Aztec societies relied on slaves, as did the ancient Indians and Chinese. But it was the Portuguese who began the African slave trade in the early 1440s.

THE AFRICAN SLAVE TRADE

Portugal was short of people to work the land and saw black Africans as an ideal source of labour. To begin with, these slaves were Africans caught by other Africans who sold them to the Portuguese at a string of forts and trading posts established along the western coast of Africa. By 1460, about 800 slaves a year were being shipped to Portugal and, remember, these 'slaves' were frightened kidnapped men, women and children. North African Arab traders soon saw the money in slavery and, throughout the fifteenth century, shipped slaves seized in central Africa to markets in Arabia, what is now Iran and the Indian continent. The Spanish soon started trading in people too, but for over 100 years, the Portuguese were the main slave traders.

THE TRADE WITH SPAIN

Having colonized parts of South America in the late sixteenth century, the Spanish wanted slaves to cultivate the land. The obvious choice were the native South Americans themselves, such as the Aztecs, but, unfortunately, many of them were soon wiped out by the diseases brought by the Spanish. Because these diseases were new to South Americans, their bodies didn't have any natural resistance to them. Not only that, they were worked so hard under such hot and humid conditions that many died of exhaustion. The obvious solution was to buy African slaves off the Portuguese, already used to working hard under such conditions. Britain entered this terrible trade when it won the contract to supply African slaves to the Spanish through the British South Sea Company in 1713.

NORTH AMERICAN SLAVE TRADE

The first African slaves brought to North America came to work in Jamestown, Virginia – the first permanent, successful English colony to be set up in North America – in 1619. They were few in number and had the same legal rights as some Native American and white servants, though there was nothing they could do about having been kidnapped and taken from their homeland against their will. As the number and size of plantations grew in the southern colonies of North America, the 'need' for slaves grew too, though many slaves in the north were used for domestic chores.

TREATING HUMANS LIKE ANIMALS

Quite apart from the cruelty of the very idea of slavery itself and the dreadful overcrowding and conditions in the ships bringing them from their homelands, there were other appalling practices in the keeping of slaves. Some slaves were branded like cattle – they had their owner's brand burnt into their skin with a hot iron. Others were forced to wear slave collars, or walked in shackles to stop them running away. Owners killing slaves was not uncommon either. Despite this, slaves in North America were supposed to have some basic rights. By the time of the American War of Independence, the rights and responsibilities of the slave owner and slave were clearly laid out, even if they were often ignored.

AN END TO THE TRADE

When looking back from the twenty-first century to the eighteenth- and nineteenth-century slave trade, it's difficult to imagine why every decent person didn't think that it was a terrible thing and should be abolished. The traders themselves might have been motivated by greed, along with the big plantation owners who were getting cheap labour, but what about all ordinary men and women? Surely they were horrified by what was going on? There were certainly 'kind' slave owners who treated their slaves 'well', but what on earth were they doing keeping slaves in the first place? This is often the problem with looking back in history. It's easy to forget that people then were brought up in a totally different climate and culture to how we are today. For most white Europeans, slavery seemed a normal part of everyday life. It was fortunate, therefore, that there *were* men and women who believed it was wrong even then, and spoke out against it.

MR SHARP AND MR STRONG

Granville Sharp was born in Durham, England, in 1735. His grandfather was the Archbishop of York and his father was an archdeacon, but Sharp didn't want a career in the church. After a brief spell in the clothes trade, he became a clerk in the civil service. His whole world was turned upside down one day, though, when he was staying in his brother's house in Wapping, East London. The year was 1765, and Granville Sharp's brother was a surgeon. One day, a man was brought to the house because he'd been pistol-whipped – very badly beaten with the butt of a pistol. His name was Jonathan Strong and he was a black slave, brought over from Barbados. The man who'd beaten him was his master, David Lisle. Granville Sharp took Jonathan Strong to St Bartholomew's Hospital where he remained for four months – yes, *four months* – to recover from his serious injuries.

TAKING ACTION

Amazingly, when Jonathan Strong was discharged from hospital and fully recovered, his master Lisle paid two men to go out and recapture him! Granville Sharp was so horrified that he took Lisle to court, claiming that since Jonathan Strong was in England where there were no slaves (there were only slaves in the colonies), Strong was no longer a slave so couldn't 'belong' to anyone. Although it took the courts until 1768 to agree with him, the case gained plenty of publicity and opened up the debate of the rights and wrongs of the slave trade. Granville Sharp, meanwhile, took up the causes of men in similar positions to Jonathan Strong, such as Thomas Lewis and James Somersett.

VOICES AGAINST SLAVERY

Having long since resigned from the British civil service, because he supported the American colonists in their fight for independence, Granville Sharp decided to form *The Society for the* **Abolition** *of the Slave Trade*, with his young friend Thomas Clarkson. Born in 1760, Clarkson had become a strong believer in the abolition of slavery after winning a 1785 Cambridge University essay competition entitled 'Is it right to make men slaves against their will?'. Both he and Granville Sharp were members of the Church of England but of the twelve members on the board of their newly formed society, nine were **Quakers**. Clarkson managed to get hold of leg shackles, branding irons and slave collars to show audiences the true horrors of slavery, and wrote a pamphlet urging the end of the slave trade.

WILLIAM WILBERFORCE

The society persuaded the MP for Hull, a man called William Wilberforce, to speak on anti-slavery issues in the Houses of Parliament. Wilberforce was to become one of the greatest names in the anti-slave trade movement. In May 1789, he gave his first anti-slavery speech in parliament. In 1791, he introduced a bill to abolish the slave trade. It was defeated by 75 votes. In 1805, Wilberforce managed to get the House of Commons to pass a bill making it illegal for any British subject to transport slaves. Unfortunately, this was then stopped by the House of Lords so didn't become law. In 1806 – after a change of government – the Abolition of the Slave Trade Bill was passed by the Lords and went back to the Commons were the voting was 114 votes for the bill and only 15 against. On 25 March 1807 it became law.

A LONG WAY TO GO

The immediate effect of this new act was that any British captain found with slaves on board his vessel was fined £100 for each and every slave. £100 was a lot of money and, multiplying it by the number of slaves, could leave a captain bankrupt. This was seen as a good way of deterring them from continuing their evil trade. In truth, some British captains carried on as slavers and simply threw slaves overboard, leaving them to drown, if they thought a British naval ship was coming. But this wasn't the only reason why the work of the anti-slavery movement wasn't over. All this law did was to ban Britain taking part in the trading of slaves. It didn't make slavery itself illegal.

1807 saw Granville Sharp and Thomas Clarkson join with a man named Thomas Fowell Buxton to form *The Society for the Mitigation and* **Gradual** *Abolition of Slavery*. The reason why they thought abolition should be gradual rather than immediate was they believed that the slaves should have time to be educated and prepared for their freedom. This was also the official view of the *Anti-Slavery Society*, founded in 1823. Others believed that all slaves in British colonies should be freed immediately.

THE WOMEN SPEAK

A number of women's anti-slavery societies were formed by women such as Elizabeth Heyrick, Anne Knight, Mary Lloyd and Elizabeth Pease. 1824 saw Elizabeth Heyrick publish a pamphlet arguing just this point: that slaves should be granted their freedom there and then. It was wrong to wait. The first anti-slavery society to actually call for the immediate freeing of slaves was the Sheffield Female Society in 1827. Many women even boycotted sugar produced on slave plantations, and this captured the imagination of the British public. In 1830, the Female Society for Birmingham called for the *Anti-Slavery Society* to campaign for the immediate end to slavery at their national conference – and, if not, the Female Society would withdraw all the funding they gave them. The Female Society were brilliant fund-raisers for the anti-slavery cause, and to lose their donation would be a big blow. At the May 1830 conference, a new campaign for the immediate freeing of slaves, led by one Sarah Wedgwood, was agreed. In 1833, the Abolition of Slavery Act became law.

THE AMERICAN CIVIL WAR

Although the USA abolished the slave trade just one year after the British, in 1808, slavery itself wasn't abolished throughout the country until 1865. In fact, the country was divided – north and south – by the slavery issue, and this led to the American Civil War (1861–65). In 1861, eleven southern states broke away from the United States, declaring themselves to be the Confederate States of America. These were the states which relied on slave labour to work on their plantations and keep their economy thriving. The newly elected president of the United States, Abraham Lincoln, said that the Confederates could not leave the Union, and that it was an illegal act. War broke out. In the end, the Confederates were defeated. More than 600,000 people had died but more than 4 million slaves were freed.

NEXT?

Over time, the slave trade and then slavery itself was outlawed in country after country across the world. As South American colonies gained freedom from their Spanish and Portuguese masters, most of these newly formed independent republics granted their slaves freedom at the same time. In 1926, the League of Nations adopted the International Slavery Convention, clearly stating that no forms of slavery should be allowed to exist. In 1948, these sentiments were incorporated into the United Nations' Universal Declaration of Human Rights. Although it is impossible to say with any certainty that there are no slaves left anywhere in the world today, we can say that the world-wide trade in millions of human beings is, thankfully, no more.

THE LEGACY OF SLAVERY

Possibly the biggest effect on the world by slavery, and its final abolition, is the huge spread of black Africans and their descendants across the globe. There are, for example, over 34 million black people living in the USA today. It is unlikely that there would be nearly that number if their ancestors hadn't been seized from their homelands and forced to work on American soil. Without US slavery, there might have been no segregation laws – separating white people from black people – and no civil rights movement, led by the likes of Martin Luther King Jr, fighting for their abolition (which you can read about in *WOW! Ideas that Changed the World*). Many people simply take for granted that South American and Caribbean countries have always been populated by black people, but this isn't true. It's another example of descendants of black African slaves and freed slaves building new lives away from home. The rich variety of different black cultures, but with common roots, is one of the few good things to have come from this most dreadful of trades.

THE FIRST WORLD WAR

28 JUNE 1914, SARAJEVO, BOSNIA

Archduke Francis Ferdinand is being driven through the street of Sarajevo in his open-top carriage. He is on home ground. Bosnia is a part of the mighty Austro-Hungarian Empire, and the archduke is next in line to the thrones of both Austria and Hungary. One day, the people on these streets and in these houses will be his subjects . . . unless . . . unless . . . A man steps forward as the carriage nears. His name is Gavrilo Princip. Before anyone can stop him, he raises a weapon at the archduke, steadies his hand and fires.

A WAR TO END ALL WARS?

As their names suggest, no two wars have had more impact on the world than the First and Second World Wars. The First World War (1914–18) began as a local conflict between Austria-Hungary and Serbia but became a full-blown European and, later, *world* war when Russia and the USA were dragged into the conflict. At its height, there were thirty-two different nations fighting: Germany, Austria-Hungary, Turkey and Bulgaria, known as the Central Powers, against the Allies made up of twenty-eight nations in all, including Britain, France, Russia and the

USA. Sometimes referred to as World War I or the Great War, the First World War was also known as 'The War to End All Wars'. Sadly it wasn't.

A SHOOTING AT SARAJEVO

On the surface, the cause of the outbreak of the First World War was the murder of Archduke Ferdinand in Sarajevo. His assassin was a Serb nationalist and hater of the Austro-Hungarian Empire. This made the murder a political assassination and an international incident, and wars had been fought for a lot less in the past. The actual reasons for the war, though, were much more deep-rooted than that.

TAKING SIDES

At the beginning of the twentieth century, Germany was in dispute with Britain and France over colonies in their African empires, and more and more countries began pouring more and more money into their armies and navies in preparation for a war that they knew would come, sooner or later. They also began to take sides, forming alliances 'in case of war' which were more likely to actually *cause* war! The Triple Alliance consisted of Germany, Austria-Hungary and Turkey, and the Triple Entente was made up of Britain, France and Russia. After a few false starts, involving Germany and France in dispute over Morocco, and the Balkan Wars (1912–13) in which Italy declared war on Turkey, Archduke Ferdinand was killed in June 1914 and the First World War began a month later.

DECLARATIONS OF WAR

It officially began on 28 July 1914, with Austria declaring war on Serbia, and Russia mobilizing some of its troops ready to fight Austria. The Germans then told the Russians that if they joined the war, Germany would fight them and, when Russia refused to demobilize immediately, Germany declared war on them on 1 August. Two days later, they declared war on France. To get to France, the German army would have to march through Belgium, but Belgium wouldn't give them permission. When Germany said that they were coming through anyway, Britain declared war on Germany on 4 August 1914 (because they'd signed a treaty promising to defend Belgium's **neutrality**).

THE 'BRITISH' ROYALS

Kaiser Wilhelm (nicknamed 'Kaiser Bill' by the British) was not only Emperor of Germany and King of Prussia, but was also the son of the late Queen Victoria's eldest daughter. King George V, on the other hand, who was on the throne of *England* during the First World War, was the son of the late Queen Victoria's eldest *son* – which meant that the two heads of state were not only on opposite sides in the war but were also first cousins who shared the same granny! The British monarchy's family name at the time was Saxe-Coburg-Gotha. Fearful that it might not go down too well with the German-loathing British public, it was quietly changed to Windsor in 1917.

MANY FRONTS

The First World War was fought on many different fronts (areas of conflict). On the eastern front, Russia seized Poland as early as 1914 and looked like it was going to seize Hungary too, until combined German and Austrian forces finally forced the Russians out, causing terrible casualties. On the western front, the Germans planned to swoop through Belgium and take control of France but, after the Battle of Flanders at the end of 1914, the war on the western front stopped being a war of armies-on-the-move and turned into what the First World War is most famous for: trench warfare.

TRENCH WARFARE

On the western front, enemy faced enemy in their facing lines of **trenches**, with a barbed-wire strewn muddy no man's land in between. If an enemy bullet or shell didn't kill you, disease could, and 'going over the top' (of your trench) left you wide open to enemy fire. Huge numbers of lives were lost over gains of just a few feet of land. At one stage, the ordinary British troops on the front line were described as 'lions led by donkeys'. Throughout 1915 the Allies were on the attack, at Neuve Chapelle in March, Vimyu Ridge in May and Loos in September. The Germans were on the **offensive** in May at Ypres (which British veterans pronounced 'wipers' – it's actually pronounced something like 'eepr'). It was at Ypres that poisonous gas was used for the first time. In December of 1915, the Commander-in-Chief of British Forces, Sir John French was replaced by Sir Douglas Haig. 1915 also saw British forces invading Mesopotamia and landing in Gallipoli (in Turkey), which had to be evacuated in January 1916.

BLEEDING FRANCE WHITE

1916 was the year that German 'bled France white', starting with an attack at Verdun on the western front in February and continuing ceaselessly until June, but still failing to gain any significant ground. The Allies began their offensive in the area of the Somme river, slowly pushing forward from July to November. It was here that tanks were used in warfare for the very first time, not that they were particularly effective under such muddy conditions. A French attack at Verdun, meanwhile, helped regain the little land Germany had taken.

THE USA JOIN THE FIGHT

Early in the war, German submarines blockaded Britain, attempting to sink any ships going in or out. On 7 May 1915, they sank the passenger liner the *Lusitania*, killing a number of US passengers. On 16 March 1916, the French steamer the *Sussex* was sunk in the English Channel, killing yet more US passengers, but still the USA didn't actually enter the war. On 31 May 1916, British and German naval forces engaged in fighting off Jutland. Although the British fleet suffered more losses, they gave the German fleet such a pounding that it stayed in port for the remainder of the war! Further German submarine attacks on civilian ships carrying US passengers led to the USA entering the war, on the Allies' side, on 6 April 1917. This was an important turning point for the Allies whose troops were battle-weary and demoralized.

REVOLUTION IN THE RANKS

Russia wasn't only fighting a war on the eastern front, but had its own troubles back home. In March 1917, the **Tsar** and his family were overthrown and a new, liberal government came to power in Russia. This government wanted to continue the war, however, so soon found itself overthrown too! The new revolutionary rulers were the Bolsheviks – **Communists** who immediately pressed for peace. (You can find out more about communism in *Wow! Ideas that Changed the World*.) Fighting stopped in December 1917 and Russia signed a peace treaty in March 1918. They were out of the war.

MORE GAINS AND LOSSES

Near the start of 1917, the Germans retreated to the north of the Somme to a new line of pre-prepared defences called the Hindenberg Line. In April, the Allies launched an attack on Vimy Ridge and, although they successfully captured it, the loss of human life was enormous. As a result, there was mutiny in the French ranks, with many soldiers fleeing. From July to November 1917 came an Allied advance from Ypres in the direction of the French coast. This became known as the Passchendaele offensive (after a village in Flanders) and the British suffered heavy casualties – which is 'war speak' for saying that many were killed or terribly injured.

THE ITALIAN FRONT

Meanwhile, in Italy, the Italians (who were members of the Allies against Germany) were holding up well against the enemy until October 1917. This was when combined Austrian and German forces attacked at Caporetta, forcing the Italians to fall back with terrible deaths and casualties. An Allied Council was set up to try and coordinate a more unified approach and French and British soldiers were sent to the Italian front to try to help out.

AMERICANS UNDER FIRE

In March 1918, the Germans began their final push for victory on the western front – at least, that's what they hoped it'd be – and it began very successfully. In less than three months, they'd retaken all the land that the Allies had gained in 1915, but what they'd failed to do was break through the Allied line of forces. It may have retreated, but they hadn't got through it to attack from behind. And the

Allies had reinforcements, and not just any old reinforcements. They were reinforced with US troops, fresh and ready to fight (and under enemy fire for the first time in June 1918). All Allied troops were now under the command of the Chief of General Staff, Frenchman General Ferdinand Foch (pronounced Fo*sh*, if you want to say the name out loud).

THE TURNING TIDE

On 15 July, the Germans began an offensive on Rheims. The Allies responded with an attack on Marne and, by the beginning of August, the Germans had retreated to their line of defence. By the end of August, the British had broken through it. The US then went into action as a separate, independent army alongside the French. The tide had turned.

PEACE BREAKING OUT EVERYWHERE

In September 1918, the Allies attacked Bulgaria which quickly agreed to peace terms and, the following month, they forced the Austrians out of Serbia. On 3 November, the Austrians signed an armistice (a truce to give up fighting until a proper, final treaty was agreed). Turkey had agreed to an armistice on 30 October.

REVOLUTION FROM WITHIN

There had always been those Germans uneasy with what was being done in their name, and the Russian Revolution had led to more outspoken anti-war feelings in Germany. When, in October 1918, the German fleet was ordered to prepare for action, there was outright mutiny and this spread from city to city right across Germany. Germany began to discuss peace with the Allies on 6 November and on 9 November Kaiser Bill was forced to **abdicate**.

AND IN THE END . . .

The First World War was lasted four years, three months and two weeks, ending at 11 o'clock on the 11th day of the 11th month (November) 1918, with the armistice signed in the forest of Compiègne. It had been fought on land, sea and, for the first time, in the air, with Zeppelins dropping bombs and bi-planes engaging in **dog fights**. There were over 37 million casualties of soldiers alone and another 10 million or so civilian casualties, caught up in the war in one way or another. Over 8.5 million soldiers died. The Russians suffered the worst casualties, not only in sheer numbers but also as a percentage of the numbers of troops who fought. Around 1,700,000 were killed, 4,950,000 were injured and 2,500,000 missing or prisoners. That was over 76 per cent of the number of Russians called up to fight. The USA, whose intervention in the war helped lead to the Allied victory, had, on the other hand, casualties of only 8 per cent.

BAD TO WORSE

The world after the First World War was a different place. A whole generation of young men had been killed, injured or seen such horrors that life could never be quite the same. There really was a feeling that the world had 'learnt its lesson' and that there would never be warfare on such a grand scale again – that it really had been 'The War to End All Wars'. Then 1918 and 1919 saw a deadly Spanish Flu epidemic spread across the world, killing even more people than the fighting had done. Some people saw this as 'divine retribution', a punishment from God for the First World War.

HERE WE GO AGAIN

War memorials sprang up in towns and villages across Europe, and 11th November became Remembrance Day, a day when those who fought, died or were injured were remembered. Meanwhile, Germany began to rise from the ashes of defeat. The agreements reached in the peace treaties were never properly enforced, and it wasn't long before Germany began growing into a military power again, with aggressive ideas that would lead to disruption and disorder in other parts of Europe . . . and finally to the outbreak of the Second World War.

THE SECOND WORLD WAR

29 SEPTEMBER 1938, LONDON, ENGLAND

British prime minister Neville Chamberlain steps out of the aircraft and waves to the assembled crowd. There is a cheer. He walks over to a group of waiting reporters and, speaking into a microphone, raises a document above his head. 'I have here a piece of paper,' he begins, and goes on to explain that it's a copy of the Munich Pact signed by – amongst others – Adolf Hitler, and how it will mean 'peace in our time'. He is wrong. In less than a year, Britain will be at war with Germany.

ALL NATIONS TOUCHED BY WAR

The Second World War was fought from 1939 to 1945, following the rise of the **Nazis** in Austria and Germany, led by Adolf Hitler. On the one side were the Allies, led by Britain, the **USSR**, France, China and the USA, whilst on the other were the Axis powers headed by Germany, Italy and Japan. By the end of the conflict most nations in the world had been touched by the war in one way or another.

TAKING TERRITORIES BY FORCE AND FEAR

Before the war itself broke out, Germany, Italy and Japan had been throwing their weight about a bit. The Japanese conquered Manchuria (a region of north-east China) in 1931 and then invaded the rest of China in 1937. The Italians conquered Ethiopia in Africa in 1935–36. The Germans and Italians entered the Spanish Civil War (1936–39) on the side of the **Fascists**. Then in 1936–37, treaties signed between Germany, Italy and Japan created the Rome-Berlin-Tokyo Axis, which is how they, and their right-wing allies, came to be known as the Axis powers. Then, in March 1938, Germany 'annexed' Austria, making it a part of German territory. The Chancellor of Germany and leader of the Nazi Party, Adolf Hitler, was himself an Austrian. In September that same year, Germany seized Sudetenland, which was a part of what was then Czechoslovakia along Germany's western border.

APPEASING THE AGGRESSOR

Britain and France were unhappy with what was happening but, with Germany armed to the teeth again, and a reluctance to go to war again so soon, they accepted that acts such as the annexing of Austria were 'internal affairs', and that the outside world shouldn't interfere. The USA, meanwhile, had passed a law which meant that it must remain neutral and mustn't aid any sides in foreign conflicts. Britain and France tried to reason with Hitler and his allies, with a policy of 'appeasement'. (Appeasement really meant compromise: granting Germany concessions they may not really have a right to, in the hope of keeping a wider peace.) The result was the Munich Pact, signed by Germany, Italy, Britain and France in September 1938. In it, it was agreed that Czechoslovakia should give up its Sudetenland region to Germany (after all, it contained 3.5 million German-speaking people), in return for the guarantee that Germany would not take any more Czech territory.

BRITAIN DECLARES WAR

In March 1939, Germany completely ignored the pact and marched into Czechoslovakia anyway. The Italians conquered Albania the following month. Horrified, Britain and France were eager to get the USSR on their side in case trouble escalated even further. In August, however, the USSR signed a 'non-aggression' pact with Germany, each agreeing to leave the other alone! On 1 September 1939, Germany invaded Poland. Hitler was confident that Britain and France wouldn't dare interfere. Now, *he* was wrong. On 3 September, Britain and France declared war on Germany.

POLAND AND BEYOND

After the Germans' successful invasion of Poland, with the fall of its capital city, Warsaw, on 27 September, little more happened until 1940. Then, in May of that year, Germany invaded Denmark and Norway. The British and French went to help Norway but had to withdraw when France itself was invaded in June. With the British people unhappy with the failure of the Munich Pact and all that had happened since, Chamberlain's government fell and was replaced by a government made up of members of all political parties, headed by the new prime minister, Winston Churchill. Germany's invasion of Belgium in May 1940 led to one of the most famous evacuation of troops in British history, from Dunkirk, a northern French port. During the evacuation, British and French troops, who'd been fighting German advances, were saved by a flotilla of ships which travelled back and forth across the English Channel. It was made up of everything from small fishing boats and pleasure craft to military vessels, brought across by a mixture of sailors and civilians. This makeshift navy of 'little ships' saved the lives of over 337,000 men and quickly passed into folklore. Overrun by German forces, and with Italy now declaring war against the Allies, France was forced to sign an armistice with Germany, but the French resistance movement fought on, backed by the Free French movement, lead by General de Gaulle in London – French soldiers still fighting against the Axis.

BRITAIN STANDS ALONE

With the USSR having signed a non-aggression pact, the USA committed to staying neutral, and much of continental Europe overrun by Germany, Britain pretty much stood alone against the enemy from 1940–41. Then, in August 1940, began the Battle of Britain. The German airforce, the Luftwaffe, launched bombing raid after bombing raid on Britain. They started them in daylight

but, having lost almost 2,000 aeroplanes, decided that night-time raids, under the cover of darkness, might be better! Churchill said of the British Royal Air Force fighter pilots who faced them: 'Never in the field of human conflict has so much been owed by so many to so few.' Despite inflicting terrible damage and loss of life on London, Coventry, Liverpool, Hull and many other cities, Britain did not surrender, and the bomb attacks became much fewer and far between. In 1940 the Greeks fought off an invading Italian force but, along with Yugoslavia, they were defeated by German forces in 1941, despite British assistance.

ENTER THE USSR AND THE USA

In June 1941, Germany, somewhat foolishly, now felt confident enough to attack the USSR, which meant that the latter could no longer remain 'non-aggressive' but would have to come out fighting against the Axis powers. Meanwhile, USA public opinion was more and more in favour of joining the war, on the side of the British. Then, on 7 December 1941, Japan bombed the US navy base at Pearl Harbor, Hawaii, and declared war on Britain and the USA! On 11 December, Germany and Italy also declared war on the USA!

AFRICA, THE NEAR EAST AND ITALY

1940 saw war raging in Africa and the Near East, with German forces under Rommel facing British forces under General Montgomery (**aka** 'Monty'). Here, a European war was being fought on the soil of its colonies. Monty's most famous victory was at El Alamein. When General Eisenhower landed British and US troops in Morocco and Algeria, the Axis forces were forced to surrender in 1943.

Allied forces now crossed from North Africa and invaded Italy. On 25 July, the Italian Fascist leader Mussolini was overthrown, and ended up being strung from a lamp-post by fellow Italians. On 13 October, under a new government, Italy declared war on Germany. Germany tried invading but were, eventually, defeated in April 1945.

VICTORY IN THE EAST!

The Allies' victory at El Alamein and Eisenhower's landing in Morocco and Algeria, along with the Germans' failure to capture the city of Stalingrad in the USSR are considered, by brainy military experts who understand such things, as the turning points in the war. Now the USSR went out and out against the Axis forces, killing or capturing 330,000 enemy forces at Stalingrad alone. They forced them out of Russia, entered Yugoslavia, freed Poland and Austria and entered Czechoslovakia and, from there, entered Germany itself and headed for its capital city, Berlin.

D-DAY!

Plans, meanwhile, had been underway to liberate the west. After mass air raids on Germany from 1940 onwards, the invasion was launched under the control of the now supreme allied commander, General Eisenhower, on 6 June 1944. It was codenamed 'D-Day', and began with landings on the beaches of Normandy. By the end of September, the Allies had entered Belgium and the Netherlands and liberated most of France. When the USSR reached Berlin, Germany surrendered unconditionally on 7 May 1945. Adolf Hitler is believed to have committed suicide.

THE WAR AGAINST JAPAN

The fight against Japan, however, was not yet over. Early in the war, the Japanese had control of the Philippines, Malaya, Thailand, Hong Kong, Burma and Singapore. In 1943, the Allies' attack against Japan was split three ways: Lord Mountbatten in Burma (what is now Myanmar), Admiral Nimitz in the Central Pacific and General MacArthur in the South West Pacific. By May 1945, Burma was almost completely back under Allied control and the Allies were making gains elsewhere in the region when the war against Japan came to a sudden and terrifying end. To shorten the war, the USA dropped two newly invented atom bombs on two Japanese cities: Hiroshima and Nagasaki. (You can read about this in *Wow! Discoveries that Changed the World.*) The Japanese formally surrendered on 2 September 1945.

THE HOLOCAUST

From the moment the Nazi Party came to power in Germany in 1933, it began to discriminate against and persecute Jewish people. They lost jobs in the civil service and other important positions and Jewish doctors were only allowed to treat Jewish patients. One night, in November 1938, hundreds of synagogues in Germany were set on fire, the windows of Jewish shops were smashed and thousands of Jews were arrested. This event became known as *Kristallnacht* – or the 'Night of Broken Glass'. Hundreds of thousands of Jewish people fled the country, yet many more remained. The more countries Germany invaded, however, the more Jews it had within its borders. They were forced to wear yellow stars and armbands to distinguish them, but much worse was yet to come. In 1941, the Germans planned to implement 'the final solution': the murder of all Jews in death camps. Most of these death camps were built in occupied Poland, and it was here that Jews were deported – many in railway cattle trucks – from German-occupied territory. The most infamous of these camps was called Auschwitz. The total number of Jewish people murdered by the Nazis is estimated to be about 6 million by the end of the war.

THESE WHO HAVE FALLEN

One of the big differences between the First and Second World Wars was that bombing raids (by aeroplanes and rockets) brought the war to civilians in those countries not even occupied by enemy forces. It also saw the introduction of a whole new type of weapon – the atom bomb. And then there were the sheer numbers of people who had died. There were 25 million members of the military and 30 million civilians, in addition to the almost 6 million people murdered in the Holocaust. These are such large figures, it's almost impossible to think of them as dead human beings. The post-war world was also left with the birth of two superpowers – the USA and the USSR – the threat of nuclear weapons, and the formation of the **United Nations**, intended to prevent many of the original types of problem that led to the Second World War.

TO THE MOON AND BACK

21 JULY 1969, THE MOON

The world watches and waits with bated breath as American astronaut Neil Armstrong is about to become the first human being to set foot on a patch of ground that is not a part of planet Earth. Grainy black-and-white pictures are beamed from the moon to Earth as Armstrong reaches the bottom of the ladder of the lunar module *Eagle* and steps onto the moon's surface. Armstrong speaks to the world via his radio microphone set inside his helmet: 'This is one small step for man,' he says. 'One giant leap for mankind.'

THE FANTASY OF SPACE

Frenchman Cyrano de Bergerac is a famous character, with a very big nose, in a play written by Edmond Rostand in 1897. What's less well-known is that he really existed. He was a seventeenth-century writer and his works included what we now call science fiction. He wrote a story about a trip to the moon in 1656. De Bergerac wasn't the first to do this – Ancient Greek writer Lucien wrote about an imaginary trip to the moon in his *True History* (which wasn't true *or* history), over 1,800 years ago – and he certainly wasn't the last, either. Two hundred or so years after De Bergerac, fellow Frenchman Jules Verne (famous for his *Around the World in 80 Days*) wrote a book called *From the Earth to the Moon* in 1865. In 1901, Englishman H. G. Wells wrote *The First Men in the Moon*. Thereafter, comic book after comic book and film after film followed with science fiction adventures of men, women and children travelling to the moon and beyond.

SOME SERIOUS SUGGESTIONS

It wasn't just the writers of fiction who were interested in the possibilities of reaching the moon. In 1903, the Russian thinker Konstantin Tsiolkovsky published a book called *A Rocket into Cosmic Space*. He was one of the first people to argue in print that the only way of getting through the Earth's atmosphere and out into space was with a rocket. In 1919 an American, Robert Goddard, published a paper called *A Method of Reaching Extreme Altitudes*, proposing a project to fire a small, unmanned (peopleless) rocket to the moon. He built a number of very small rockets, some of which went faster than the speed of sound.

THE ADVANCES OF WAR

It was the hard facts of war rather than dreams of space travel that brought the development of rocket science forward in leaps and bounds. German student Wernher von Braun had always been fascinated with the idea of rockets and space flight. He and a group of friends built and launched their own small rockets in Kymmersdorf, near Berlin. In 1932, their activities aroused the interest of the German military. The good news was that von Braun soon found himself the head of an experimental rocket station . . . the bad news was that these rockets weren't to take anyone to the moon but were to be flying bombs. The result were the V2s, which regularly landed in Britain, killing and injuring hundreds of people during the Second World War.

ESCAPE!

At the end of the Second World War, with Germany defeated, von Braun gave himself up to the US army, willingly sharing the secrets of his new rocket technology. Soon the Americans had him making rockets for them, but still only as weapons. In 1955 he became an American citizen, but 1957 was an even more significant year for von Braun, because this was the year that the **Soviets** launched the world's first space satellite – and soon the space race between the USA and the USSR would begin.

MACHINES IN SPACE

The Soviet satellite *Sputnik 1* was launched by the USSR in October 1957, and orbited the Earth. *Sputnik 1*'s full name was *Iskustvennyi Sputnik Zemli* which is Russian for 'Fellow World Traveller of the Earth'. *Sputnik 2* was launched a month later and, this time, carried a dog named Laika to see how living, breathing creatures survived in space. She was fine, until her oxygen supply ran out. By January 1958, the USA had their satellite *Explorer 1* up in orbit too. The Soviets launched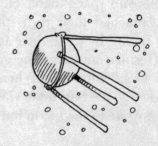

Sputnik 3 in May of that year and the space race was hotting up.

THE AMERICAN REACTION

Eager to make sure that the USA wasn't left behind in the space race, US President Dwight D. Eisenhower passed the National Aeronautics and Space Act in 1958 which, amongst other things, created NASA (the National Aeronautics and Space Administration). In 1958, both the Soviets and the Americans were unsuccessful in attempts to launch and land unmanned probes on the moon which could send back valuable information and pictures. The Soviets succeeded in September 1959 with their *Luna 2* probe. The world's first pictures of the dark side of the moon (never seen from here on Earth) were taken by a camera on board *Luna 3* launched in October of the same year. Although the USA's *Ranger 7* probe took some stunning pictures of the moon's surface in July 1964, giving the first really clear close-up pictures of the moon, the Americans were concerned that, in the space race to the moon, the Soviets had achieved all the major 'firsts' so far. In February 1966, the USSR's *Lunar 9* made the first soft landing on the moon – in other words, it didn't crash and get damaged.

A FISTFUL OF FIRSTS

NASA had launched their Lunar programme a month after Soviet **cosmonaut** Yuri Gagarin became the first person in space on 12 April 1961. The USSR seemed well ahead in the race. Especially when cosmonaut Valentina Tereshkova became the first woman in space as early as 16 June 1963. In May 1961, NASA had started the Apollo programme: an attempt to land a person on the moon and bring him – all the astronauts in their programme were men – safely back to Earth. The programme was launched by US President John F. Kennedy.

APOLLO

The Apollo missions began in 1967, and with tragedy. On 27 January 1967, three American astronauts, Virgil Grissom, Edward White II, and Roger Chaffee, died in their space craft when it was still on the ground, during a run-through of take-off procedures of Apollo 1. A fire burnt up all the oxygen in the capsule and they couldn't breathe.

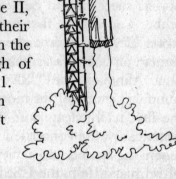

APOLLO ELEVEN – TO THE MOON!

The launch vehicles for Apollo missions – the actual rockets which blasted the men and machinery out of the Earth's atmosphere and into space were *Saturn V* rockets. These were designed by the former German V2 rocket scientist Wernher von Braun, including the rocket, launched from Cape Canaveral, which was to begin the first flight to the moon: *Apollo 11*. Once in space, the

rocket section served no
purpose and was jettisoned
from the remaining sections:
the command module
Columbia and the lunar
landing module, *Eagle*.
Whilst Neil Armstrong
and Edwin 'Buzz' Aldrin

took the *Eagle* to the moon's surface, astronaut Michael
Collins piloted the *Columbia*. If anything went wrong down
on the moon, Collins's instructions would have been to fly
home alone. The lunar module landed in a flat area called
the Sea of Tranquillity – though there was no water in it –
and the landing site was called Tranquillity Base. The *Eagle*
was on the moon for just 21 hours
and 36 minutes, of which
Armstrong and Aldrin spent 2
hours 31 minutes out and
about exploring and collecting
samples. The eight-day mission
was a complete success, the
Eagle re-docking with the
Columbia command module,
before being jettisoned and all
three astronauts returning to
Earth in a tiny capsule which
landed in the Pacific Ocean.

OTHER TRIUMPHS

After Apollo 11, probably the most famous Apollo mission
was Apollo 13, launched in April 1970. Although disaster

struck and it never reached the moon, all three astronauts managed to return to Earth safely, thanks not only to their skills but also to the skills and instructions of those back at NASA Mission Control in Houston, Texas. Mission Control first became aware of the difficulties when astronaut James Lovell announced: 'Houston. We have a problem.' The problem was that an explosion had caused the command module to lose oxygen and electrical power, and the astronauts had to move into the lunar module. Thanks to some ingenious makeshift adjustments and repairs, they made it home. These dramatic and exciting events have since been retold in the film *Apollo 13*, released in 1995, with Tom Hanks in the role of Commander Lovell.

SO FEW

So far, only twelve people have walked on the moon. The first were Neil Armstrong and 'Buzz' Aldrin on the Apollo 11 mission in June 1969, and the last were Harrison Schmitt and Gene Cernan on the Apollo 17 mission in December 1972. All were American astronauts. Once the Americans had landed there, the Soviets turned their attention to other achievements in space. Since then, there have been space shuttle flights, long stays onboard space stations and unmanned probes to the planet Mars and beyond, but none of these events have quite the excitement of watching live television pictures of a human being setting foot on the moon for the very first time – or the image of the Earth itself as seen from the moon: small and vulnerable, just hanging there in space.

THE FALL OF THE BERLIN WALL

9 NOVEMBER 1989, THE BERLIN WALL, EAST GERMANY

Standing on top of the Berlin Wall, looking down into West Berlin, the small group of people can't quite believe it's really happening. They can't believe they're really here. A few days ago, anyone would have been shot dead by East German guards just trying to reach this point – many have died in the attempt in the past – yet here they are, on top of the wall – on top of the WORLD! Someone starts smashing at the wall, chipping away at the concrete. Yes! That's it! The wall must come down. East and West must unite. The crowds grow bigger by the minute. There is crying. There is laughter. There are cheers. The wall must come down . . .

AFTER THE WAR

At the end of the Second World War in 1945, Germany was a defeated country and its capital city Berlin was surrounded by Soviet-occupied territory. The city itself, however, was divided into four sectors: British, US, French and Soviet, with representatives from each sector on a governing board. The problem was that although the Soviets (often referred to as the Russians because Russia was the biggest country in the USSR) were on the winning side, and lost more troops than any other country in the war, they weren't trusted by their allies and the Soviets didn't trust them in return. The Soviets were communists, whilst the British, US and French were **capitalists**. This marked the beginning of the Cold War – not a war of battles and guns but of mistrust, spying and trying to get the upper hand.

THE BERLIN AIRLIFT

In 1948, the Soviets withdrew from the governing board of Berlin, and set up their own totally separate municipal government for their part of the city. They argued that there was no longer any reason for the British, US and French to remain in Berlin and, being surrounded by Soviet territory, the city should become totally part of the Soviet zone. They blockaded all the routes to West Berlin by road, railway and water, depriving West Berliners of food and supplies – but their plans were crushed by the Berlin airlift. The British and US flew supplies into West Berlin for eleven whole months, until the Soviets ended the blockade.

WARNING
BEYOND THIS
POINT IS THE
RUSSIAN ZONE

TWO REPUBLICS ARE BORN

As a result, the British, US and French decided that the German land they'd occupied since the end of the war should be united to create the Federal Republic of Germany (West Germany), and that their three remaining sectors of Berlin should become a part of it. This was finalized in May 1949. In October 1949, the USSR declared their occupied Germany territory to be the German Democratic Republic (East Germany) and East Berlin to be its capital city.

THE TWO BERLINS

For westerners to reach West Berlin, they had to travel through East Germany, or to fly over it, via agreed routes or 'corridors'. Life in capitalist West Berlin was much more relaxed than life in the communist East so, between 1949 and the drastic action that was to follow in 1961, 2.7 million – yes, that's 2,700,000 – fled from the Soviet-controlled East Germany to the West. More than half of these came via West Berlin. Eventually, the communist government ordered the building of a wall to surround the whole of West Berlin.

UP SPRINGS THE WALL

The wall came into being overnight on 13 August 1961. The original wall was not a true wall but was rolls of barbed wire, and the backs of people's houses (with the windows boarded and later bricked up). It was also lines of armed guards, who soon had their own watch towers to make sure than no one could escape. In those early days, though, people *did* escape. Families had been divided overnight and wanted to be together. Ways were found through cellars or other gaps in the defences until the proper wall was completed, with regular patrols and little hope of escape. The final 4-metre-high wall was 103 miles (166 kilometres) long, of which only 28 (45 kilometres) miles divided East Berlin from West. The rest of it separated West Berlin from the rest of East Germany. There were only twelve crossing points into West Berlin from East Germany, and only two crossing points between the East and West of the city, the most famous being Checkpoint Charlie.

SOVIET CLAIMS

The East Germans claimed that the Berlin Wall had been built to prevent any political or military interference from West Berlin and the West Germans, whilst it was clear to the West that it was really to keep the East Germans *in*! The East German government didn't want people getting to West Berlin via East Berlin or East Germany as a whole. In West Germany, it was possible to walk right up to the wall, and miles of it was covered in colourful graffiti. On the Eastern side, it was a different story. East Berliners couldn't get anywhere near the wall. There was an area of 'no man's land' along many of the stretches, with additional barbed-wire fencing, ditches and even tank traps to be crossed before anyone could get close to the actual Berlin Wall itself. That didn't stop people trying to escape

– many succeeded, but over a hundred were killed in the process.

THE GORBACHEV BROOM SWEEPS CLEAN

In 1985, a man named Mikhail Gorbachev became the General Secretary of the Communist Party in the USSR and, in 1988, President of the USSR itself. Unlike many Soviet leaders before him, he seemed genuinely interested in giving power and democratic rights to the people, rather than letting the top-heavy communist government keep a tight control on all aspects of Soviet life. He introduced two ideas to the USSR: *perestroika*, which is Russian for 'restructuring' and *glasnost* – 'openness'. He wanted to restructure the economy and to have openness in political and cultural life. He withdrew Soviet troops from disputed territories, signed arms treaties with old Cold War enemies, transferred power to legislatures elected by the people not run by the Communist Party, and gave Eastern bloc countries new freedoms.

THE END OF THE WALL

As a result of these incredible changes, in the summer of 1989, the former Eastern bloc Hungarians allowed East Germans to travel through Hungary if they wanted to get to Austria or West Germany. Power in East Germany was

crumbling. In one fell swoop, the Berlin Wall had become completely irrelevant. There was a much easier way out of East Germany than trying to cross into West Berlin! Come autumn, the former Soviet-backed East Germany government was teetering on the brink of collapse. Then, on 9 November 1989, the unthinkable happened: people started climbing up onto the Berlin Wall and knocking great chunks out of it – and nobody tried to stop them.

AFTER THE WALL

In the end, East Germany officially helped with the removal of the wall and, in 1990, the two countries were reunited as one: the Federal Republic of Germany, run along western lines. In the same year, Mikhail Gorbachev was awarded the Nobel Prize for Peace. In 1991, the USSR

– one of the most powerful empires in the twentieth century, if not history, collapsed and was no more. The world would never be the same again, and the fall of the Berlin Wall was a symbol of this incredible change.

THE FREEING OF
NELSON MANDELA

11 FEBRUARY 1990, NEAR VICTOR VERSTER PRISON, SOUTH AFRICA

Crowds of reporters and photographers surge forward as a tall, distinguished figure in a suit walks towards them along the dusty road leading from the prison. Grey-haired, and even slightly frail-looking, is this really the same man whose familiar, younger face stares determinedly from posters across the globe? Here, after almost 27 years in jail, is the first glimpse of Nelson Mandela, free at last.

A MAN OF IDEALS

Nelson Mandela was imprisoned in 1964 for 'sabotage and subversion' against his home country of South Africa. His real crime, however, was being a black person in a country where by far the most people were black, but were ruled by the small minority of whites. Even membership of the political party, the ANC (African National Congress), which Nelson Mandela joined in

1944, had been made illegal in 1960 – the same year as the Sharpeville Massacre, in which around 70 black demonstrators were killed.

IN THE BEGINNING

Most white South Africans today are Afrikaners (sometimes called Boers), descended from settlers who originally came from the Netherlands. Britain wanted to rule South Africa, as part of its huge empire, but, in the late 1800s, some Afrikaners promoted the idea that they were 'the chosen people'. Britain defeated the Afrikaners in the First and Second Boer Wars, but two South African Afrikaner republics were granted self-rule by the British in 1907: the Transvaal and the Orange Free State. But soon the whole of South Africa was an independent country under Afrikaner rule. South Africa fought alongside Britain in the First World War, which upset many Afrikaners. In the Second World War, the loyalties of the Afrikaners were divided. Many supported Britain and the Allies, but many agreed with the anti-black ideas of Germany's Nazi Party. In 1948, the Afrikaner National Party, led by Daniel François Malan, won the election based on the issue of dividing whites from non-whites. Apartheid was born.

THE RISE OF THE NATIONALS

A year later, the National Party classed people as 'white', 'black', 'coloured' or 'Asian' and introduced the Group Areas Act. This law made sure that where you lived and worked, and what rights you had (or, more to the point, *didn't* have) depended on the colour of your skin. The whites ruled supreme, with the best houses, jobs and freedoms, and non-whites were treated like second- or third-class citizens. This became known as apartheid, from the Afrikaans language, meaning 'apart-hood'. But, in the 1990s, all this was about to change.

THE YOUNG MANDELA

Nelson Mandela, the son of a Xhosa-speaking chief, was born in 1918 in a village near Umtata, South Africa, in what is now Eastern Cape province. He went to the University of Fort Hare and quickly became a part of the political struggle against racial discrimination, and was kicked out in 1940 for his part in a student demonstration. He managed to finish his degree by taking a **correspondence course** with the University of South Africa and then went on to study for a law degree. He became more and more involved with the ANC – a nationalist movement made up of people of all skin colours – which hoped to bring about democratic change in South Africa.

A CAMPAIGN OF DEFIANCE

In 1952 the ANC launched the Defiance Campaign, in which protesters defied the apartheid laws across the whole of South Africa. Also in 1952, Nelson Mandela became one of the ANC's deputy presidents and national-Volunteer-in-Chief. Worried that the ANC would be banned, its leaders put something called the 'M' plan into operation. (The 'M' actually stood for Mandela!) The plan reorganized the ANC into small groups of members who could, in turn, encourage ordinary people to join the struggle against apartheid. The idea behind it was that a large number of small groups of volunteers would be much harder for government forces to **infiltrate** and put a stop to than one big, official organization. Mandela also opened up the first black law practice with his friend Oliver Tambo. Efforts to have him struck off the list of practising lawyers failed.

TAKING UP ARMS

As time went on, Mandela and others began to think that an armed struggle might be an important part of the fight against apartheid. Talking and demonstrating simply wasn't enough. In 1956, he found himself charged with treason, for his part in the various anti-apartheid, anti-government campaigns, at a trial which was to last five years. He was found innocent and acquitted.

MASSACRE!

In 1960 the ANC, along with another group called the PAC (Pan-Africanist Congress), called for a day of demonstrations on 21 March, right across the country, to protest against South Africa's pass laws. The pass laws strictly limited the movement and employment of black people, and meant that they had to carry their identity papers ('reference books') with them all the time. It was as a part of this day of demonstrations that a large crowd of

men, women and children gathered outside a police station in Sharpeville, Johannesburg. Some black people started burning their identity papers, some threw stones, and the (white) police opened fire. They kept on firing even when the terrified protesters started running away. Around 70 black men, women and children – figures vary from 67 to 72 – were killed and over 180 injured.

A STATE OF EMERGENCY

Uproar and outrage in the black community was immediate. There followed everything from peaceful protest marches and strikes to all-out riots, right across South Africa. A state of emergency was declared and over 18,000 people were arrested. The ANC and the PAC were banned, but continued in secret as illegal organizations. Countries around the world were horrified by what the South African government was doing, and South Africa's actions were officially condemned by the **United Nations**.

89

SPEAR OF THE NATION

Following the massacre, the now-banned ANC finally gave up their commitment to non-violence and a military wing, called 'Umkhonto we Sizwe' ('Spear of the Nation') was founded in December 1961, with Nelson Mandela as its commander-in-chief. Without getting official permission to leave the country – something all black people had to do – he went to the neighbouring country of Algeria for military training. When he returned to South Africa in 1962, he was arrested. At his trial, he conducted his own defence and began by saying, 'I detest racialism because I regard it as a barbaric thing, whether it comes from a black man or a white man.' He was sentenced to five years in prison.

SENTENCED TO LIFE

Soon, many of Nelson Mandela's ANC colleagues were arrested too, and he was put on trial alongside them for sabotage, treason and violent conspiracy. Found guilty, he was sentenced to life imprisonment in June 1964. For the next 18 years he was a prisoner in a tiny cell on Robben Island where conditions were very strict and harsh. Amazingly, Nelson Mandela and other political prisoners managed to keep in touch with apartheid groups secretly. He even managed to write most of his autobiography *Long Walk to Freedom* in captivity and to have it smuggled off Robben Island. Later, he was moved to another maximum-security prison, Pollsmoor Prison, near Cape Town. Finally, he was moved to Victor Verster Prison. Meanwhile, he'd become a symbol for the whole anti-apartheid movement, and world leaders and ordinary people protested for his release.

A NEW BEGINNING

It was as a result of this huge pressure, from home and abroad, that the then (white) president of South Africa, F. W. de Klerk, finally lifted the ban against the ANC and released Nelson Mandela in February 1990. After years of protest, de Klerk finally brought about a whites-only referendum in 1992, asking white people to back his plans to make a new constitution, giving proper rights to black people. Over two-thirds of the voters overwhelmingly voted for free elections for *everyone*. In 1993, both Mr de Klerk and Mr Mandela were awarded the Nobel Prize for Peace.

PRESIDENT MANDELA

In 1994, South Africa's first free elections brought the African Nation Congress to power, with Nelson Mandela as South Africa's first black president. 'Mr. Mandela has walked a long road and now stands at the top of the hill,' said F. W. de Klerk. Nelson Mandela himself described the election as: 'For all South Africa, an unforgettable occasion.' Nelson Mandela's release from prison was something that most people had thought was very unlikely. A black person being elected president of South Africa was an event that many people in the world had never dreamed was possible.

Glossary

abdicate – to give up being the monarch

abolition – the act of abolishing or ending (in this case the slave trade or slavery)

aka – 'also known as'

American Patriots – Colonists loyal to America, rather than Britain

barbarians – the Roman name usually given to anyone living outside Roman territory

capitalists – supporters of capitalism, an economic system based on the private ownership of capital (money, property, etc.)

coats-of-arms – design in the shape of a particular shield, representing a particular family

Communists – members of, and believers in, a society where, in theory, everything belongs to the state and profits are shared amongst everyone

Confederate – a member of the breakaway Confederation of southern American states

correspondence course – an educational course where student and teacher communicate by mail

cosmonaut – the Soviet name for a space traveller (what the Americans call an astronaut)

despotism – the rule of a tyrant

dog fights – close-up fights between two or more aeroplanes

empire – a group of countries with the same ruler, in this case Rome

Fascists – followers of Fascism, a right-wing movement against democracy and liberalism, and for strict authority

flying shuttle – a device used in weaving for crossing the threads

forum – a place for open discussion

governor – Roman ruler of a foreign territory

gradual – over time (not straight away)

infiltrate – to secretly gain entry into

Kaiser – German Emperor

Loyalists – those American colonists loyal to Britain

mass-produced – goods manufactured in large numbers to the same design

Mediterranean area – countries bordering the Mediterranean Sea, a large inland sea between South Europe, North Africa and South-west Asia

mutinies – revolts against those in charge (often regular troops rising up against officers)

naval blockade – tactic preventing ships or supplies getting in or out

Nazis – members of the **fascist** National Socialist German Worker's Party, with racist and brutal ideals

neutrality – the not taking of sides

offensive – attacking (rather than defensive)

papyrus – paper made from a fibrous plant

philanthropists – people, usually wealthy, who perform charitable and benevolent acts to help others

phonic alphabet – an alphabet in which the letters go together to create written versions of the sounds required to say words

province – an area outside Rome itself, but controlled by Romans

punctuation – symbols (not letters) used to divide up sentences, showing who's speaking, for example, when writing

Quakers – members of the Society of Friends. Christians who reject rituals and at whose religious meetings anyone can speak

Renaissance – flowering of the arts in Europe, from the fourteenth to sixteenth centuries, inspired by the works of the Ancient Romans and Greeks

republic – a country or state which elects its government and which doesn't have a king, queen or emperor

senators – members of the Senate, Rome's governing council

Soviets – people of the USSR

transported – taken abroad to a penal colony

trenches – a system of large ditches used to protect troops at the front line

Tsar – the Emperor of Russia

unifier – someone who 'unifies', brings people together

Unionist – an American loyal to the United States of America and against the breakaway Confederation in the south

United Nations – an association of states pledged to world peace and security, working throughout the world through such organizations as the World Health Organization (WHO) and the United Nations Children's Fund (UNICEF). The UN's security council is responsible for sending UN troops (drawn from different member states) to police 'hot spots' across the globe

USSR – the Union for Soviet Socialist Republics, or Soviet Union, made up of a variety of communist republics, including Russia (no longer exists)

Index